DORSET IN WINTER

DORSET *in* WINTER

ROGER HOLMAN

HALSGROVE

First published in Great Britain in 2010

Title page photograph:
Melbury Wood
Looking down on Melbury Wood.

British Library Cataloguing-in-Publication Data
A CIP record for this title is available from the British Library

ISBN 978 0 85704 051 0

HALSGROVE
Halsgrove House,
Ryelands Industrial Estate,
Bagley Road, Wellington, Somerset TA21 9PZ
Tel: 01823 653777   Fax: 01823 216796
email: sales@halsgrove.com

Part of the Halsgrove group of companies
Information on all Halsgrove titles is available at: www.halsgrove.com

Printed and bound in Italy by Grafiche Flaminia

INTRODUCTION

When wild geese honk high of nights, and when women without seal-skin coats grow kind to their husbands, you know winter is near O. Henry

When Halsgrove asked me to photograph another book on Dorset, my first reaction was, no, I have completed eight over a period of nearly 20 years and it's about time I hung up the camera and stayed in bed until a sensible hour arrived. In 2007 when I completed *Dorset – The Glorious County*, I said to Rosemary 'that is the last book I shall do'. She smiled knowingly as wives do and obviously didn't believe me. Needless to say she was right. I have completed two more small books since then and now this one. I suppose it was a combination of a challenge and the prospect of having a good reason to be out and about in this wonderful county during my favourite season that changed my mind.

For a lot of people, winter is the period between autumn and spring that has to be endured and can't pass too quickly, but not for me. I love the winter. I just love the snow when we get it, bringing back memories of childhood days playing snowballs and sledging when of course the snow was deeper and more frequent (or is that nostalgia?). Snow is the great leveller. It covers everything without fear or favour making even the ugly and mundane appear attractive. A manicured lawn looks no different than a ploughed field under a few inches of snow. I also love the bright frosty mornings, how sometimes the hoar frost clings to every twig and how ice patterns form on windows and other flat surfaces.

Yes, of course, there are times when the weather is foul but to sit in front of a roaring log fire while the rain patters on the window, seems to me to be an experience to be treasured. If you happen to be a reluctant gardener, the bonus of not having a lot to do in the garden during the winter season is particularly attractive.

The weather generally smiles benignly on Dorset in winter although 2009/10 did have its moments, especially in the north of the county, and some of the Poole Harbour shoreline did freeze over but that is an extremely rare occurrence.

In comparison with Dorset's inland landscape, the 70 miles of shoreline change far less over the seasons, in fact it is not always possible to say at what time of the year a particular picture has been taken.

Through this journey of winter in Dorset, I would like to think I could have persuaded a few folks who had thought otherwise that winter is a season to be celebrated and treasured. Wrap up well and enjoy it!

I must thank Rosemary for the tolerance and support she gave me and some good photographic friends of mine, Tony Bates, Kay Browning, Ron Holmes and Roger Lane who generously allowed me to use a few of their pictures of places I had not covered. Their images are credited.

Roger Holman, 2010

Golden Cap

Golden Cap is the highest sea cliff in southern England standing at 618 feet. Much erosion has occurred over the years exposing the upper crest of greensand which is probably responsible for its name. This and the profile of the ridge at the summit of the hill make it easily identifiable.

Golden Cap
Golden Cap seen from the east with Seatown in the
foreground and Lyme Regis in the distance.

Right: **Opposite Golden Cap**
From Seatown looking east.

Beaminster

Beaminster lies in the great hollow of surrounding hills. Sir Frederick Treves complimented the town by recording "it is a clean, cheerful, self-respecting county town without pretensions and without brick suburbs now but happily still retains an attractive atmosphere." It has one of Dorset's tallest church towers from where in 1685 the quartered remains of some of Monmouth's ill-fated army were hung for all to see.

Cattistock Hunt

The Cattistock Hunt gathers at the start of the day's riding with a traditional glass of port and sausage rolls which appear to be free to all who turn up. They no longer hunt foxes but follow a trail laid by soaking a rag in fox's urine.

Upcerne
The great children's author and travel writer Arthur Mee wrote of Up Cerne
"lying among the downs smiling to itself like a child in hiding, delighted that the
highroad passes so near yet misses it." It is small indeed but does boast a fine gabled
manor house built about the beginning of the seventeenth century.

Left: **Colmer's Hill**
Colmer's Hill to the west of Bridport, was named after Reverend James Colmer at the beginning
of the nineteenth century and is a landmark that most people will remember as they travel
the A35 to the West Country. The pines on the summit were planted about 100 years ago
and now new ones have been added to replace those lost to age and decay.

Upcerne

Right: **Minterne House**
Minterne House is in a beautiful location at the base of a valley of wooded hills.
It is the home of the Digbys who have connections to the Duke of Marlborough
and the Churchill family. The gardens and lake are spectacular.

Minterne Magna
Minterne Magna's church of St Andrew.

Minterne Magna

Little Minterne Hill
Snowy lane, Little Minterne Hill. For me, this type of scene conjures up childhood memories
of winters when more snow fell and these normally familiar places became a new world to explore.

Left: Minterne Magna

Holnest
The medieval church of St Mary.

Left: From Little Minterne Hill

Above and left: **Blackmoor Vale**
Overlooking the Blackmoor Vale.

Mid Dorset
From the A352 near Watts Hill.

Left: **Buckland Newton**
North of Buckland Newton the hills flatten
out into the Blackmoor Vale.

Beech Trees
I believe the landscape is so enhanced
by these isolated clumps of beech trees the
farmers have left untouched, especially when
they are standing on the summit of a hill.

Marnhull
Hardy named this village Marlott and made it the birthplace of his heroine
Tess of the D'Urbervilles. Also in the story the Crown Inn became the Pure Drop Inn.

Right: **The Giant, Cerne Abbas**
Cerne Abbas seems to have changed little over the years but its main claim to fame is of course the Giant cut
into the hill overlooking the village. It is 180 feet in height and needs scouring out every few years to stop it
from disappearing. In 1868 the local clergy wanted it left without cleaning because they felt it was corrupting
the local population! It was supposed to lure childless couples up its escarpment on moonless nights.

From Crown Point
near Cerne Abbas

Left: Gold Hill, Shaftesbury
Gold Hill, Shaftesbury must be one of those images
that everyone instantly recognises due to the Hovis
advertising campaign in the 1970s.

Gold Hill
Recently Hovis re-enacted the original advert with Olympic gold
medallist Victoria Pendleton replacing the boy on a bike.

Sturminster Newton Mill

There has been a mill on this site for over 1000 years. Although not now in commercial use, it is still in working order and a tribute to the generations of millers who toiled here providing food for the community.

Right: **Fiddleford Mill**

Arguably one of the most picturesque mills in Dorset. It is connected to a very early manor house dating back to the 1370s which reputedly was used in smuggling days. It looks as if little has changed over the centuries.

Fiddleford Mill Pond

The water in the mill pond is very calm, enhancing the reflections and
colours of early morning light. I was very much attracted by the serenity
of the scene helped by the little boat moored under the tree.

Right: Milton Abbey and School

Milton Abbey and school rest contentedly by the lake in a valley of wooded
hills. The original village of Milton Abbas was built around the house and
abbey but Lord Milton disliked having such close neighbours so between
1775 and 1786 he had the village dwellings demolished and rebuilt nearby
where they now stand elegantly either side of a wide main street.

Bulbarrow
Apart from the stunning vistas Bulbarrow is renowned for its
bluebell woods.

Left: **From Bulbarrow Hill**
This is looking west from Bulbarrow Hill. The streams and
brooks from this area feed the River Stour and from where there
are commanding views to the north and west overlooking
The Blackmoor Vale.

Courtesy Roger Lane

Melbury Abbas
The view from the Dorset/Wiltshire border looking north into
Wiltshire just before the road drops down Zig Zag Hill to Cann Common.

Left: **Wingreen**
This picture is taken on the Wilts/Dorset border where the distinctive landmark of
beech trees at Wingreen can just be glimpsed on the horizon.

Ashmore

Ashmore's claim to fame rests with the fact that it is the highest village in Dorset, standing at over 700 ft above sea level. It is also famous for having a large duck pond lined with clay to retain the water. Recently all the silt that had built up over the years was removed and the base re-puddled. Because of the altitude, the relationship between evaporation and condensation is such that little water is lost. These ponds are called dewponds.

Right: **Clayesmore School**

Clayesmore is an independent school for boys and girls founded in 1930, set in a 62 acre campus.

Courtesy Steven Holman

Fontmell
Down

Fontmell Down
Young and old enjoy the snowy slopes.

Fontmell Down
Fontmell Down is situated in the north of the county and possesses stunning views over
The Blackmoor Vale. Summertime brings a proliferation of chalk downland wild flowers. It is
jointly managed by The National Trust and The Dorset Wildlife Trust.

Melbury Hill

Left: Fontmell Down
Fontmell Wood.

Overleaf: Compton Abbas
The Blackmoor Vale and Compton Abbas.

Melbury Wood
Melbury Wood looking as if the landscape has been dovetailed together.

Left: **Fontmell Wood**
Fontmell Wood in newly fallen snow.

Courtesy Tony Bates

Durweston
The village of Durweston is situated by the River Stour
on the Blandford to Sturminster Newton road.

Right: **Ackling Dyke**
Ackling Dyke is a tribute to the road building skill of the Romans.
Standing here at dusk it is not difficult to imagine Vespasian's
legions marching by on their way to Old Sarum.

Horton

The eighteenth-century Georgian church of St Wolfrida was built on the site of an earlier abbey. Beneath the tower is a memorial to the eccentric village squire, Henry Hastings, who was reputed to have eaten oysters twice a day and died at the age of 99 in 1650. He was a great sportsman whose interest in game was only matched by his desire for women.

Left: **Knowlton**

Knowlton is a deserted medieval village with this ruined church standing in the middle of a Neolithic henge monument. The chancel dates back to the twelfth century and the tower to the fourteenth. It became derelict in the eighteenth when the roof fell in.

Horton Tower

Horton Tower was built in the eighteenth century for local landowner Humphrey Sturt. There is little history written about it but the consensus is that he had it built to watch the hunt when he became too old to ride. For whatever reason, he could never have visualised that 250 years later it would be still standing and used for communications by Vodaphone. The aerials are so well sited that few people are aware of their presence.

Right: **Horton Tower**
Horton Tower from the village.

Sheep in Snow
The young lambs are obviously old enough to withstand these
conditions or else they would have been taken inside.

Right: **Cranborne Chase**
The tops of the trees eerily appear through the mist
as it rolls across the valley on a cold winter's day.

Chalbury Church

All Saints, Chalbury is a delightful thirteenth-century church with views to the Isle of Wight, New Forest and North Dorset. For two centuries a telegraph station stood nearby from where in 1805, news of the victory at Trafalgar was signalled. This was one in a line of stations situated between Plymouth and London.

Right: **Moors Valley**

Moors Valley is owned and run by the East Dorset District Council and has proved extremely popular. It includes a large lake inhabited by many species of birds not least the ubiquitous swan gliding gracefully over the water

Mannington Heath

Mannington Heath is situated just north of Wimborne. It is elevated on the
western edge enabling panoramic views to the east and is a good place to watch the
sun rise. Walking there makes it feel much more remote than it really is.

Left: **Moors Valley**

The humidity of the lake here causes ice to form quickly on the grasses making it a very photogenic subject.

Mannington Heath
Frost on fern.

Left: Mannington Heath

Mannington Heath

Right: Walking by the Stour at Dudsbury

The Stour at Parley
The river becomes wider and deeper as it approaches its destination in
Christchurch Harbour where it meets the Hampshire Avon.

Canford School

Canford Manor was owned by Lady Cornelia Wimborne before she sold it to become a school which opened on 15 May 1923. It is now co-educational with 600 pupils and a staff of 100. In 1992 the school benefited from the discovery in the tuck-shop of a rare antiquity known as the Assyrian Relief, which eventually raised £7.7 million at auction.

Courtesy Roger Lane

Chestnut Walk, Canford School
Canford boasts an arboretum.

Courtesy Roger Lane

Millstream, Canford School

Right: Stour at Canford

Hoar-frost on the Stour as it flows past Canford School.

**Winter Feed,
Little Canford**
Stock being fed at Little Canford.

Beech Avenue, Badbury

The magnificent pollarded avenue on the road to Badbury Rings was planted on the instructions of William John Bankes in 1835. Alas the trees are now reaching the end of their lives with many gaps appearing due to gales and decay. A replacement programme has been instituted with new trees a distance back from the originals but will take many years to attain their stature.

Left: **Stour Floods, Sturminster**

The Stour rarely floods as much as this. The 'No Fishing' sign that is just visible is a trifle redundant under these conditions.

Badbury Rings
Badbury Rings, now owned by The National Trust,
is always very popular with the public, particularly when
there is enough snow to make some gentle sledging possible.

Right: **Point-to-Point**
A great family day out.

Point-to-Point

The Iron Age Fort of Badbury Rings is a perfect location for a Point-to-Point meeting as the elevated rings give uninterrupted views of the whole course for the huge crowds that attend these regular events.

Point-to-Point, Badbury

Betting on the races is all part of the fun at a Point-to-Point.

Point-to-Point, Badbury

To provide an added attraction at this meeting, some of the huntsmen raced camels. The animals appeared to regard it as being a little beneath their dignity with certainly no great desire to get involved in unnecessary effort. It is doubtful whether the bookies have much idea of the outcome either.

Tarrant Crawford
The grounds of the church of St Mary, Tarrant Crawford come alive
with a sea of snowdrops as a harbinger of spring.

Left: **Portman Hunt**
The Portman Hunt supporters follow the hunt by vehicle or even on foot.

Whitemill Bridge

The late medieval Whitemill Bridge at Sturminster Marshall is arguably the most attractive bridge in Dorset. It boasts eight arches and has refuges for pedestrians. Those damaging it could have ended up with a free passage to Australia.

Pamphill

Pamphill overlooks Wimborne and has a collection of thatched
cottages which was once part of the Bankes estate.

Courtesy Kay Browning

Stour Meadows
Frost turns the mundane into a little touch of magic.

Left: **River Stour**
The winter sun setting over a tranquil Stour. There are not
many fences stretching down into the river to be seen these days.

Cowgrove
An isolated cottage looks out over a cold wintry scene.

Right: **River Stour**
Both sides of this stretch of the River Stour are owned by
The National Trust so footpaths are open to the public.

Stour Meadows
A small bridge crosses one of the streams that feed the Stour.

Left: **Stour Meadow Flood**
Early morning sunrise over the flooded meadows.

Eyebridge
This fisherman obviously believes it is worth braving the early frost to land himself a catch.

Left: **Stour Meadows**

Wood Carving
A wood carving guards the river path. I'm not sure what species it is but
certainly not a live version I would wish to encounter in the dark.

Right: **Stour Meadows**
Hoar-frost clings to the trees that dot the
meadows overlooked by High Hall.

Overleaf: **Stour Meadows**
This panoramic shot taken from the Wimborne by-pass
just glimpses the Minster on the horizon.

Stour
Swans are synonymous with the Stour, in fact it is rare not to see them when you walk the river paths.

Right: **The Minster, Wimborne**
The town of Wimborne is dominated by the Minster, parts of which date back to Norman times. It is
a magnificent building, still providing a focal point for a great number of the town's activities.

Christmas Celebrations
Even the police force join in the spirit of Christmas.

Left: **Christmas Carols**
A well attended Christmas carol service being held in the Corn Market in Wimborne.

Wimborne Pancake Race

On Shrove Tuesday a traditional pancake
race is run around the Minster grounds.
Everyone is welcome to have a go.

Holt Forest
Holt Forest is a magical place to
walk at anytime but especially
after a fall of snow.

Left and Right:
Holt Forest

The Garden

This Dorset garden is transformed with a fall of snow.

Courtesy Ron Holmes

Snow on Mahonia Leaves
The red leaves of the Mahonia shrub
jump out against the snow.

Frost Patterns

When I was a child, before most houses had central heating and certainly before the introduction
of double glazing, I was always fascinated by the exquisite frost patterns that nature chose to deposit
on our windows. This one is enhanced by being on the surface of a red car.

Frost on Pussy Willow

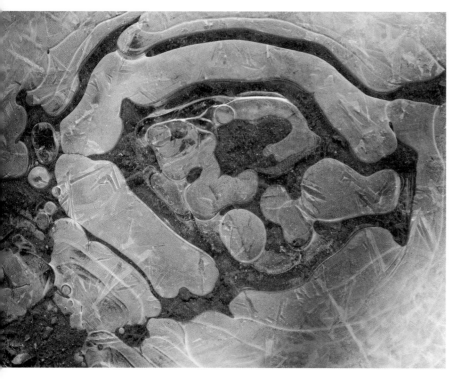

Ice Patterns
Nature unerringly freezes the water into interesting
and sometimes beautiful patterns.

Right: Hardy's Tower
Dorset has not one famous Hardy but two. The monument in this
picture is the memorial to Sir Thomas Masterman Hardy who was
Nelson's flagship captain. Thomas Hardy the author is buried in
Poet's Corner, Westminster Abbey.

Hedge Laying

These young people are learning the craft of hedge laying under the auspices of
The Dorset Wildlife Trust, which is responsible for forty two conservation areas
encompassing 300 acres. Surprisingly it employs a staff of 60, with the help of several
hundred volunteers and an annual budget of two and a half million pounds.

Right: **Osmington Mills**

Here the little stream gurgles happily over pebbles as
it reaches its destination at Osmington Mills.

Kimmeridge

Kimmeridge Bay is a wonderful place in all seasons but particularly atmospheric in winter. The famous Kimmeridge Ledges become exposed when the tide is out, and as the coast runs east/west, the sun sets over the sea at that time of year.

Left: Wool

Early morning sunrise at Wool looking over the flooded Frome.

Wareham
Poplars by the River Frome at Wareham.

Left: **Kimmeridge Waterfall**
The little waterfall at Kimmeridge will sometimes freeze
in very cold weather as it tumbles over the cliff edge.

Wareham

Wareham has a long history dating back to the days of King Arthur, still with some surviving earthworks. In the fourteenth century it was an important port, but due to the silting up of the River Frome and larger ships being built, it declined and is now the home of many sailing boats and pleasure yachts.

Right: Wareham
River Frome, Wareham.

Corfe Castle
Corfe Castle is much photographed from every angle, and with Gold Hill and Durdle Door is one of the iconic images most associated with Dorset. Built on a steep-sided hillock it seems to grow out of the hill rather than being built on top of it.

Right: **Corfe Castle**
The village of Corfe Castle shrouded in mist viewed from one of the surrounding hills. Treves wrote of it,
"a wrinkled old place in the winter of its age, lying at the foot of the castle like a faithful hound."

The Agglestone
The Agglestone Rock, situated on Purbeck Heath, is an estimated 500 ton lump of ferruginous sandstone perched on a small hillock. Folklore claims that the devil hurled it from the Isle of Wight, somewhat inaccurately because he was aiming for Corfe Castle.

Left: **Steeple**
Steeple, sheltering under the whaleback of Smedmore Hill.

Swanage Pier
The new pier at Swanage, which was rebuilt with the aid of a lottery grant, is a magnificent affair and much improved on the original. It is seen here on a chilly winter's evening.

Poole Harbour

It is very infrequently that the temperature drops and stays low enough for the water on the shoreline of Poole Harbour to freeze as it did in 2009/10. On thawing, it produced these little ice-floes.

Left: **Poole Harbour**
Ice-floes in Poole Harbour.

Canford Heath

Canford Heath, although situated on the northern edge of Poole conurbation, is strangely remote: once on the heath it is very easy to forget how close you are to civilisation.

Left: Poole Quay

Mist invariably creates mystery as this picture of Poole Quay illustrates. This could have been taken many years ago except the lamp would have been gas rather than electric.

Compton Acres

The Chinese garden at Compton Acres with late snow falling.

Courtesy Roger Lane

Avon Causeway

The Avon causeway on the Dorset/Hants border.

Courtesy Kay Browning

Christchurch River
Christchurch Priory overlooks the meeting
place of the River Stour and the River Avon just prior
to its combined journey into Christchurch Harbour.

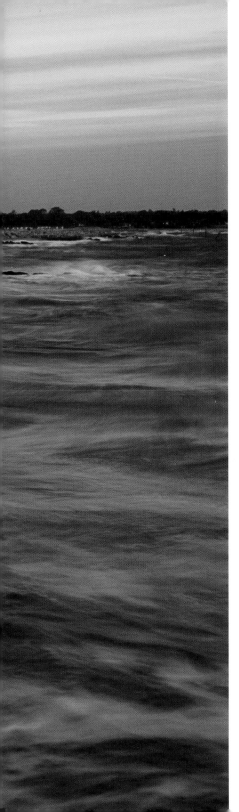

The Pulpit Rock
Waves beat over the Pulpit Rock as they have done for generations,
proof of the resilience of Portland stone.

Left: **Hengistbury Head**
An angry winter sky above Hengistbury Head where these
beach huts command extremely high prices.

Weymouth Harbour
The boat tied up at the harbour-side proclaiming the season's greetings provides a nice touch.

Studland Sand Dunes
The early morning sun has burnt off most of the frost, just leaving a few patches in the shade, reminding us that however harsh the winter spring can never be too far away.

Wild Flowers
A melody of wild spring flowers in Alderholt churchyard.